Shoplifting Control

by Read Hayes

PREVENTION
PRESS

PREVENTION PRESS, INC.
Orlando

(∞) Recognizing the importance of preserving what has been written,
it is the policy of Prevention Press to have the books it publishes printed
on acid free paper, and we exert our best efforts to that end.

Library of Congress Cataloging-in Publication Data
Hayes, Read
Shoplifting Control/by Read Hayes
p. cm.
Includes bibliographical references (p.)
ISBN (soft bound) # 0-9632762-0-4
1. Retail trade — United States — Security measures.
2. Inventory shortages — Prevention 3. Shoplifting
1. Title
HF5429.27.H39 1993
658.4'73 dc20

92-090708
CIP

British Library Cataloguing in Publication Data
Hayes, Read
Shoplifting Control
1. Title
658.47
ISBN # 0-9632762-0-4

Prevention Press
5471 Lk. Howell Rd., Ste 236
Winter Park, FL 32792 USA (407) 671-8226
10 9 8 7 6 5 4 3 2 1
Printed in the United States of America

Contents

Dedication

To all those involved in the fight against retail crime.

PART 1

The Problem

1

THE FINANCIAL IMPACT

Retail theft is as old as retail. Historical records indicate that theft incidents were reported as early as 627 A.D. One of the earliest documented accounts of shoplifting activity was recorded in 1597.

A 1698 Act of Parliament defined shoplifting as "the crime of stealing goods privately out of shops" and it dictated death for violators. There are several accounts of shoplifters who were hanged for their crimes. Despite this harsh punishment, by 1726 shoplifting was so prevalent in London that merchants asked the government for help in apprehending the thieves and a reward system was established for those citizens who turned shoplifters over to the authorities.

A significant event in the history of shoplifting occurred in 1879 when Frank W. Woolworth opened his first 5-and-10 cent store in Utica, New York, and changed the way merchandise was displayed. Woolworth took items for sale out of glass cabinets and put them on open display where customers could touch them. He also put price tags on individuals items. By tagging each item individually, Woolworth could lower his prices, as fewer employees were needed to provide service to customers. The result of these changes was two-fold — increased sales and a dramatic increase in shoplifting.

Through the years, retail and retail theft have experienced tremendous growth in terms of size and complexity. Due to the details involved with managing a successful retail operation, there is an urgent need for business people to not only understand business and economics, but also understand how retail loss occurs and how to prevent and control it.

A special note: shoplifting is a management issue. Strong, well-trained managers usually control shoplifting.

Retail theft is most often given national attention during the winter holidays largely because shoplifting provides the media with ready-made, interesting stories. However, even with this increased exposure, the problem of shoplifting goes unnoticed as a primary cause of loss in revenue. Due to the size of the retail industry, billions of dollars are lost annually to dishonest employees, vendors, and customers. Most retailers are aware of some of the loss threats that are faced daily and many retailers are familiar with effective methods and systems available for controlling those threats. However, a comprehensive guidebook has not existed, until now, that helps retailers curb rising losses caused by customer theft in the form of shoplifting.

Cost to Consumers

According to the *National Retail Security Survey*, every year retailers lose approximately $20 billion to theft committed by their customers, vendors and employees. Over $5 billion of these staggering losses is attributable to shoplifting. This problem negatively affects all consumers in at least three ways:

1. **Higher consumer prices** - merchants are forced to raise prices to cover their increase in cost of doing business (i.e.. loss of merchandise, working capital and cost of security) placing the financial burden ultimately on the honest consumer (approximately $209 per household).

2. **Overburdened criminal justice system** - many apprehended novice shoplifters and dishonest employees are referred to the already overcrowded system (police, courts, corrections). This results in the need for more tax revenue to pay for a continual expansion of the system.

3. **Lost tax revenues** - merchandise lost to theft is not converted

to profit in the form of sales for the retailer. As a result, millions in tax revenues are lost. Again, the honest tax payer must bear the financial burden of runaway theft.

Cost to Retailers

Shoplifting by customers (or customers in collusion with employees) obviously reduces company inventory levels. This non-sales reduction in inventory negatively affects the retailer in at least three ways:

1. Shoplifters of all types normally steal the most desired merchandise. Sometimes literally stripping individual stores clean of certain items. Theft activity frustrates a merchant's attempt at remaining fully stocked in desirable merchandise, actually leading to customer dissatisfaction. A situation no retailer can afford with competition being as fierce as it is today. This customer dissatisfaction is compounded when retail companies raise prices to compensate for lowered gross margins due to theft!

2. Stolen items must be replenished. And replacement costs may be higher due to the loss of special purchase deals and/or inflationary price increases. Again, the cost of replacement in any case reduces a retailer's profit per transaction. Also, the capitol used to replace stolen merchandise may have to be taken from other profitable ventures.

3. If company employees steal cash received for legitimate purchases, reported sales remain the same. However, the cash related to reported sales isn't available for inventory replacement. Inventory replacement capital must now be diverted from other areas such as expansion into new merchandise or trading areas.

Summary

The costs of retail theft are multi-dimensional. Customers, company employees and stockholders all pay for spiraling losses. Retail companies unable to identify the causes of their losses and control it, will fail to compete effectively in the tougher market ahead.

2

TYPES OF SHOPLIFTERS

Academics, law enforcement officials and loss prevention personnel have been differentiating and labeling types of shoplifters for decades, if not centuries. All groupings are based on perception and probably no one is much more accurate than another. For the purpose of this book, I have chosen to classify shoplifters into two broad categories, Professional and Amateur/Opportunist, with corresponding subcategories. The reasoning is, by examining the motives behind a theft or thefts, the methods employed and the merchandise generally taken, individuals stealing from stores can be generally categorized. All criminal groups, just like any group, actually have hierarchies. In other words, the degree of planning, sophistication, skill and financial gain realized vary widely. Keep in mind though, shoplifters can not be readily classified. The difference between one type and another is not a clear one. In fact, individual shoplifters may cross from one type to another as their motives and methods change. The point is to look for ways to reduce the negative impact any type of shoplifter has on your business. Understanding who is stealing from you, why, and how is an important first step. (See figure 2-1)

Shoplifter Classification Matrix

	Type	Motive	Methods	Merchandise	$ Impact	Violence Potential	Detection	Deter/Defeat
Professional	True Pro	Return or sell stolen merchandise for refund; primary source of income	Conceal items in elastic girdle, booster box, trash or shopping bag; may create false receipt for refund or credit	Moderate to high dollar items easy to return or sold to fence or flea market	Generally very costly	Generally low; rarely apprehended; if caught, often get released	Very well-trained agents or employee, CCTV, luck	Customer service, cabling, credible CCTV and/or EAS systems may deter
	Hardcore Pro	Return for refund or sell items to purchase drugs, liquor, food, etc.	Conceal items in elastic girdle, shopping bag, etc.. Grab and run	Usually moderate priced items refundable or sold to fence	Generally moderate to high	Moderate to high; high if previously arrested or under influence of drugs	Agents, employees, CCTV, occasionally hidden EAS	Heavy customer service, consistent store agent program
	Casual Pro (Transition Phase)	Return for refund or sell items for extra cash	Conceal items in elastic girdle, garbage bag, etc.; may switch price tags	Usually moderate priced items refundable or sold to fence	Generally low to moderate	Generally low to moderate	Agents, employees, CCTV, hidden EAS	Customer service, cabling, CCTV, EAS, store agents, bar coding
Amateur	Primary Household Shopper (PHS)	Extend household budget	Consume edible merchandise, switch price tags, conceal items in purse or shopping bag, wear apparel	Items not on basic budget, i.e. health and beauty aids, costume jewelry, fancy apparel, gifts, cigarettes	Generally low to moderate	Generally low; usually very emotional	Well trained employees, store agents, EAS, CCTV	Customer service, CCTV, bar coding, new EAS technology for demand items; possible cardboard cutout of police officer, etc.
	Impulse (Lapse in Judgement)	Varies widely; impatient with waiting; embarrassing item (condom, etc); sudden craving for item; no money; judgement impaired by drugs/alcohol	Consume edible merchandise, switch price tags, conceal items in purse or shopping bag, wear apparel	Generally small individually desired items, i.e. book, film, calculator, batteries, CDs/cassettes/tapes	Generally low to moderate	Generally low to moderate; may be emotional	Employees, agents, CCTV (all usually by luck), EAS, merchandise alarm	Customer service, EAS, CCTV, cardboard cutout, cabling, merchandise alarms
	Juvenile (1-7 years)	Too young to form criminal intent; simple desire to possess item	Consume edible items, grab and hold or conceal	Toys, snacks, food, etc.	Generally low	Low	Employees, EAS, agents, CCTV	Parental (or employee) suspension
	Juvenile (8-18 years)	Peer pressure to steal or possess certain items; can't afford desired item	Consume edible items, wear apparel, conceal item in pocket or purse, etc.	Demand items like costume jewelry, auto parts, CDs, cosmetics, etc.	Generally low to moderate	May be low to high (unpredictable)	Employees, agents, EAS, CCTV	Customer service, EAS, CCTV, cabling, merchandise alarms, bar coding
	Psychological (Kleptomania)	Very rare condition	Consume edible merchandise, conceal in pocket or purse	Items taken may be selected randomly or as a pattern	Generally low	Low to high depending on age and severity of illness	Employees, agents, EAS, CCTV	Customer service, merchandise alarms

©1993 Read Hayes, CPP

(Figure 2-1)

Professional Shoplifters

Most retail theft experts agree that individuals who steal from retailers in order to derive all or part of their pay are in the minority. But the percentages of annual theft dollars lost to professional versus amateur shoplifters has yet to be proven scientifically. Stores that carry items which have a high resale potential (i.e.. athletic apparel, cigarettes, meat, etc.) and those with very liberal cash refund policies are the most vulnerable to continued visits from professional shoplifters.

I have categorized professionals in to three subgroups based on motives, methods, merchandise pilfered, financial impact per "hit" or theft incident and the potential for violence. Gypsies and other diversion groups also fit in to the professional category.

True Pro - Like all professionals, the true pro steals to live on the proceeds gained form selling stolen goods to a fence or flea market or returning them back to the retailer for a cash refund. The true pro usually derives most of their income from shoplifting. Many do very well, making over $100,000 a year, tax-free. True professionals are considered good actors and dress and behave for the most part like legitimate shoppers. They may work by themselves, but prefer to work in teams of 2-6 people in order to create low-key diversions and scout for store detectives and non- security employees. Large purses, foil-lined purses or shopping bags, elastic girdles and socks are the preferred receptacles for concealing stolen items.

True pros steal merchandise they know can be readily converted to cash. Fences place buy orders to be filled down to sizes, brands and colors, etc. For simple steal and refund schemes, high-dollar items are the key. Often times, the true pro won't even leave a store with the stolen goods. They simply approach the customer service desk and ask for a refund or exchange. If a receipt is actually required, some professionals print counterfeit receipts using stolen "NCR" insurance premium quote terminals or computer printers. True pros blend in very well with other customers and may even make legitimate purchases from time to time. If they are somehow caught, they are very adept at convincing retailers of their innocence or readily explained lapse in judgement.

Stores frequently visited by true pros may experience heavy dollar losses. The dollar amount stolen per incident can be very high ($100-2000).

Hardcore Pro - This individual derives their income from crime of all types. Drug sales, burglary, robbery, bad checks, shoplifting and even prostitution are weekly activities. Shoplifting, because of cash refunds and flea markets, is a very attractive source of ready cash. Cigarettes, fragrances, athletic apparel, auto parts, tools, high demand CDs and cassettes are examples of frequently targeted merchandise. Hardcore pros are more likely to have a criminal record, sometimes extensive, and therefore the potential for violence may be high. In addition to possibly carrying weapons such as straight razors, knives or guns, hardcores use many of the shoplifting tools mentioned above including hollow gift-wrapped boxes with a spring-trap door. They also will carry plastic garbage bags in their pockets which they pull out and fill with items. Items are also stuffed into their elastic girdles and pantyhose (males included). Another popular method employed is known as the hit-and-run, hit-and-get, or smash-and-grab. In this scenario they generally fill their hands or bags with merchandise and jog to a waiting getaway vehicle (with its license plate removed or covered). Sometimes they actually drive the vehicle through the front doors or windows, fill-up and flee.

Casual Pro - This type of shoplifter may actually be an amateur in transition to the professional ranks as they begin to live on their earnings. The methods they use and their potential for violence also mirror those of other types of professionals. All three types of professional shoplifters combined may make up a larger percentage of all shoplifters than earlier believed. Certainly the dollars lost to these individuals are significant.

Another aspect of professional shoplifting that is important is the communication networks that evolve. Techniques for spotting security, stores that are easy targets and new ways of stealing are spread throughout communities and states. Communication between shoplifters is often much better that between retailers. Even between different stores within a single chain.

Amateur or Opportunist Shoplifters

Numerically, individuals that steal for reasons other than financial gain (pay) far outweigh those that do. Any customer (almost) at any time may steal merchandise from a retailer if they are struck with some perceived motive and perceived opportunity. This fact makes shoplifting control very, very difficult. Spotting anyone at anytime is quite a challenge. Figure 2-1 also illustrates the subcategories listed under the amateur heading. The dollars lost per theft incident, when compared with professional shoplifters, are generally low .

Primary Household Shopper (housewife, etc.) - This type of shoplifter normally steals items not on the household budget. This type of shoplifter, male or female, occasionally or habitually steals items they probably can't afford. Cosmetics, costume jewelry, fancy apparel, deli-meats and Christmas gifts are some of the most frequently pilfered items. The PHS also tends to switch tickets or merchandise containers, again, to reduce the impact on their household spending. The most common way this type of shoplifter steals is by simply concealing items in a bag, pocket or purse. They will also wear or eat unpaid for merchandise. The negative financial impact the PHS causes per incident is generally low. Like all amateur shoplifters, the potential for violence varies with the individual. Most, when apprehended, do not use force to resist but may be very emotional. Their reactions ranging from argumentative to remorse.

Impulsive Shoplifter - Just about every retailer has apprehended a customer for theft that was clearly a result of a momentary lapse in judgement. This scenario best describes the impulse shoplifter, the largest group of shoplifters. This group is actually your customer base. An individual that suddenly (or not so suddenly) perceives a need to possess something and the opportunity to take it without payment. This may occur once in an individual's lifetime. It may also occur repeatedly, or, hopefully, never. A recent emotional event, impatience at waiting in a checkout line, reluctance at having an embarrassing item such as condoms rung up, or the sudden desire to possess a certain item and no way to pay for it may trigger an impulsive theft. These items are normally concealed in a pocket, bag or purse. The dollar amount of individual theft incidents are usually low, but the year end total may be staggering. This type of shoplifting may well pose the greatest challenge for the merchant. They must try and prevent impulsive theft acts with good customer service and often technology such as article surveillance, cabling and merchandise alarms. Like other amateurs, their reactions to apprehension are unpredictable.

Juvenile Shoplifters - Certain types of stores experience a significant amount of loss caused by persons under the age of 18. Age appears to be an important way of distinguishing between what motivates a young person to steal. As a general rule, children under the age of eight are presumed to be unable to form criminal intent. Obviously every child is different. But juveniles, regardless of their specific age, who aren't yet capable of comprehending the ramification of dishonest activity must be considered separately from children who can. Very young children simply grab items they want and must be supervised by an adult. Juveniles who are capable of forming criminal intent may be motivated by peer pressure to actually steal or more frequently to possess a particular item they can't afford. Minors of all socio-economic backgrounds are susceptible. Examples of frequently stolen merchandise include: costume jewelry, auto parts, compact discs or cassette tapes, cosmetics or name-brand apparel. Their potential for violence again depends on the individuals involved in stealing and apprehending. The financial loss per incident is generally low to moderate.

Psychological - Kleptomania is both rare and misunderstood. How much or frequently someone steals is less important than what is taken, the eventual use of stolen items, where the theft(s) occur, and finally, the capacity of the subject to recall his or her acts. The theft of apparel, obviously the wrong size (and not for resale or for someone else), or the theft of a piece of jewelry from a friend combined with no recollection of the incident may indicate kleptomania. The per incident and annual financial impact of this type of shoplifter is believed to be relatively minor. Likewise, the potential for violence is considered very low.

Summary

Again, it is difficult at best to classify shoplifters into neat categories. But by examining motives, methods and merchandise, shoplifters can be better controlled.

3
PLANNING FOR PREVENTION

Preventing shoplifting in your stores involves the implementation of various countermeasures. These countermeasures can take many forms. For the purposes of this book, they are broken down into People, Policies, Programs and Systems.

Loss Control Countermeasures

Retail organizations exist to make a profit. Therefore, when designing risk control countermeasures, the security specialist should keep several factors in mind.

Cost-effectiveness - Any loss control program (or part of the program) should prove cost-effective over a prescribed period of time. The total cost of security must be kept to the minimal amount required to control losses. Most retailers express their cost to control shrinkage as a percentage of sales. According to the 1992 *National Retail Security Survey*, the average is between 0.15 - 0.34.

The cost of control can range from almost nothing (loss control procedures) to moderate cost (employee awareness training programs), to high cost (placing EAS systems in distribution centers and all stores). All of these programs may be cost-justified based on the threats that a retailer faces, but the security specialist should think in terms of least-cost techniques and sound management principles before recommending that sophisticated security hardware be used. These may well come later, particularly for high-loss retailers.

Redundancy - The company employee responsible for loss control should keep in mind that systems designed to protect very high-risk assets should have back-up security systems in case of primary system failure. For example, perimeter and internal alarm systems should by separated in case one system fails.

Teamwork - While planning the loss control program, security specialists should take into account the fact that there may be policies, personnel, and equipment inside and outside of their control that must be altered or eliminated. When possible, these factors must be identified and made a part of the action plan and budgeting process. Senior management must be made aware of the situation and a teamwork approach should be taken to resolve these issues. Working relationships between the loss control department and other departments must not be hindered.

Both security and management executives should be sensitive to each other's goals. Total access to items enhances the tendency to buy them. However, this practice also guarantees tremendous shrinkage. Many retailers start off with a few control procedures and practices, and move toward more control as losses continue to mount. It is possible to work together to accomplish the ultimate goal of increased profitability.

Customer Convenience and Perception - Store planners use store layout and fixture schemes to induce customers to buy more of their merchandise. Also, the smart retailer strives to make their customers' shopping experience a convenient and pleasant one. As the loss prevention program is designed, the security specialist should work with store operations and merchandise display personnel to reach a happy medium between displaying all merchandise on the sidewalk and locking everything up.

The appearance of security practices and equipment should also be considered during the loss prevention program planning phase. Some customers or employees may consider a security practice or piece of equipment offensive, many won't notice it at all, and still others will be deterred from committing theft because of the

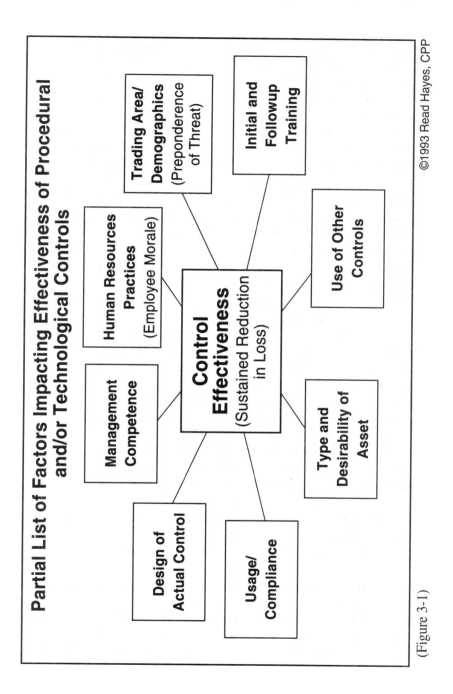

Partial List of Factors Impacting Effectiveness of Procedural and/or Technological Controls

(Figure 3-1)

practice or equipment. Again, negative perceptions of a program or system should be weighed against economic need or personal safety.

Bar coding is an example of a system that decreases the time a customer spends at the cash register, while enhancing inventory control.

Deterrence - All loss control programs include five primary techniques: prevention, control, detection, investigation and recovery. Programs and systems are primarily designed to deter people from stealing not detect them, although most good prevention systems or programs will do both. In order to effectively deter most people from stealing, most research identifies four critical factors:

Certainty - The higher the certainty that if an individual steals from a particular retailer, there exists a high probability of detection and apprehension, the more likely most people considering theft will be deterred. Also this concept may include the certainty that if merchandise is stolen, it will be rendered useless. New fluid and mechanical tags, when tampered with, stain or break pilfered items for this purpose. This factor also includes the certainty of punishment.

Severity - If caught, the possibility of severe punishment may have some deterrent effect on certain individuals. However, certainty of capture and punishment seems to play a larger role than the severity of threatened punishment.

Celerity - The swiftness of both detection and punishment also appears to help determine the level of deterrence. The quicker someone is caught and subsequently punished, the better the deterrence realized.

Communication - All three of the above factors must not only be maximized, but communicated to those we wish to deter. In the case of shoplifting, the retailer must strive to spread the word: "If you steal from me, you **will** be caught and quickly punished."

Labor Requirements - Loss control procedures or programs may require an increase in the labor force or may divert employees' attention from primary work functions to loss prevention. These factors must be considered and planned for. Many security systems actually reduce labor intensity by simplifying procedures or by assuming functions formally handled by employees or outside

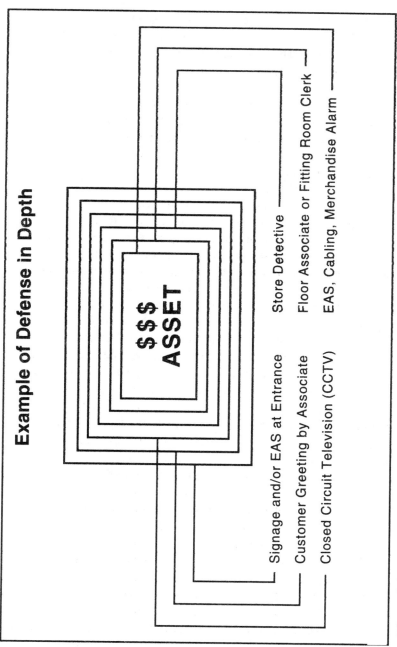

Example of Defense in Depth

$$$
ASSET

Signage and/or EAS at Entrance
Customer Greeting by Associate
Closed Circuit Television (CCTV)

Store Detective
Floor Associate or Fitting Room Clerk
EAS, Cabling, Merchandise Alarm

©1993 Read Hayes, CPP

(Figure 3-2)

contract agencies. EAS and CCTV recording systems take over some functions that may have been previously provided by security personnel. They also allow more freedom of display.

Time Sensitivity of Countermeasures - Many procedures or security systems become obsolete annually or even monthly because of new technology, sociological changes, or new court rulings. Therefore, retailers should consider countermeasures timeliness as a part of their program design. A retailer should not, however, wait indefinitely before implementing needed policies and equipment.

Program Manageability - Another factor to be considered during the design phase, is the ability of executives in charge of the security function and their staffs to effectively manage the loss prevention program. Before attempting to implement a costly, sophisticated program, the personnel involved should be carefully selected and trained. Individuals in supervisory roles must have demonstrated technical proficiency and leadership qualities, or the best-designed program in the world is doomed to minimal effectiveness.

No Guarantees - Retailers at all levels should realize that there is no such thing as an infallible security system. Incidents will occur and losses will take place. (See figure 3-1) The key is to prepare for and attempt to reduce adverse incidents, and reduce the negative effects of previously uncontrolled losses.

Defense in Depth - The most effective way to minimize shoplifting loss is to layer countermeasures in depth. (See figure 3-2) By placing several physical and psychological barriers between the threat (our customer) and the asset (our merchandise) we are able to accumulate delay time. In other words, by slowing a would-be thief down, the probability of their being discouraged or detected increases rapidly with time.

4
PEOPLE

The use of people to control losses is perhaps the most important loss prevention method and can be the most expensive one. Because of these two factors, this chapter is dedicated to this very important topic. All employees of any retail organization are responsible for controlling profit-draining loss. However, senior management generally designates one individual to be responsible for the administration of a loss control program. This individual may handle security duties in addition to other responsibilities or as their primary responsibility. Additional full or part-time individuals, whose main function is security, may be employed by the retailer or may be provided by an outside contract agency.

In-House Employees

This section provides insight into the most common loss prevention positions held in retail operations of various sizes and their role in loss control. For the purpose of this book, titles or specific job positions will be used interchangeably, since there are many common names for each position.

Director (Vice President) of Loss Control - Every group needs a leader. For the security department, the director (or the vice president) is responsible for implementing and managing company loss control functions in larger retail companies. This individual normally reports to the CEO or high-level vice president to ensure that top decision-makers are kept abreast of loss control efforts and shrinkage problems. This reporting level is also important in maintaining company-wide credibility for the loss control department and its efforts. Loss control must be viewed as a **priority** issue by all company employees.

Building on experience and education, the director sets loss control goals that fit into the overall corporate goals and designs the loss prevention program to accomplish these goals. In larger chains, subordinate managers implement and run the loss prevention program and the director acts as advisor and counselor to these subordinates to ensure and enhance the effectiveness of the program and the managers' efforts and abilities. To accomplish this, the director stays abreast of new control techniques and technologies by attending conferences, reading security journals and books, and exchanging ideas with peers (networking).

The primary role of the loss control director is to provide the direction and resources needed for cost-effective security.

Shortage Control Committees - In an effort to get key company executives involved in reducing shrinkage, committees are formed at store and corporate levels to study the problems the company is experiencing and to ensure that loss control procedures are implemented and followed.

Loss Prevention Staff - Depending on the size and type of retailer, the security staff can consist of one employee or hundreds. The staff may include a variety of personnel that have different responsibilities.

Plainclothes Agents - Retail operations that gross more than $25 million in annual sales may employ some type of in-house loss control specialist. Plainclothes agents are very effective at curbing losses from shoplifters. It is very important that individuals chosen for plainclothes agent positions be thoroughly trained.

Each retail operation should have a complete training course set up for all personnel who are authorized or expected to detect and detain shoplifting suspects (See figure 4-1). A qualified consultant should be able to recommend the specifics for creating such a training workshop. Another available option is to hire graduates of a high-quality retail/security training course. Also, be aware that there is an interactive computer training simulator on the market that is used to train store detectives. These simulators, when used in conjunction with a comprehensive security curriculum of approximately 100 hours, teach trainees the complexities of detecting, surveilling, and apprehending shoplifters. The simulators provide the trainers with reports that indicate the trainee's discretionary judgement skills and aggressiveness. Different retail organizations have different titles for these detectives; retail protection specialist, agent, operative and detective are the most common. It is important to provide quality, documented training; competitive salary and benefits; a suitable title; and senior management support of loss control personnel. This allows the retailer to attract and retain the high-quality personnel needed to implement and run an effective loss prevention program.

Uniformed Guard - Some chains use guards who wear blazers or uniforms and station them at the front of the store or allow them to patrol in order to deter theft and serve customers. It is recommended that guards be part of a loss prevention program in some very high-loss situations, but not be considered a prime theft deterrent.

Fitting Room Attendant or Store Monitor - Courteous, alert individuals should be assigned as fitting room attendants/store monitors whenever possible. Store monitors can promote goodwill for the company while deterring theft. Usually, monitors report to the store manager, although they are trained and motivated by loss prevention personnel.

Outsourced Personnel

Uniformed Security Guards - Many local, regional and national companies exist that provide businesses with armed or unarmed

LOSS PREVENTION TRAINING INSTITUTE (LPTI) / BASIC COURSE
(Level 1)

Day 1
Intro. to the course
Intro. to the Retail Industry
Intro. to Retail Loss Prevention
Problems Retailers Face Today

Day 2
Laws that Affect: Our Company, Our Jobs, and Our Customers
Our Policies on External Theft: Shoplifting, Refund Fraud, Electronic Article Surveillance

Day 3
Physical Security
Shoplifting Detection
Shoplifting Surveillance

Day 4
Shoplifting Surveillance
Report Writing
Review for Quiz 1

Day 5
EAS Systems
Quiz 1
Shoplifting
-apprehension
-escorting
Employee Awareness
Individual Evaluations (PM)

Day 6
Processing
Report Writing
Courtroom Testimony

Day 7
Civil Liabilities, Bad Stops, Case Studies
Decision Making
Privileged for Counsel Reports
Final Exam Review

Day 8
Final Exam
Employee Theft
Professionalism
Computer Testing

Day 9
Computer Testing
Oral Board
Awareness Presentations
Emergency Procedures

Day 10
Computer Testing Make-Up
Awareness Presentation Make-Up
Oral Board
Graduation

(Figure 4-1)

guards. These guards may be used to monitor specific locations during emergency situations such as power failure and special events (i.e.. new store opening, large sale, celebrity visit), or used on a routine basis as a form of theft deterrent. The retailer should verify all training claimed by the guard company and scrutinize the guards sent. Ground rules must be established as far as detention of theft suspects and patrol procedures, since most contract guards are **not** qualified to detect and apprehend shoplifters or dishonest employees.

Retailers should ask for and contact retail client references of any outside agency offering security personnel before securing their services. A contract should also be drawn up and thoroughly reviewed by the retailer's corporate legal counsel before starting the service.

Non-Security Employees

As previously stated, all employees of the company should be trained to prevent theft and waste. These employees are **the** key to low shrinkage.

Senior Management - The front line of any retail operation provides leadership and direction to the company in terms of what is to be done and how it should be done. The primary loss prevention role of senior management is to approve, endorse, and adhere to the security program. An endorsement by senior management legitimizes the personnel, procedures, and systems used to reduce shrinkage, and ensures that security remains a significant priority in the company.

Senior management can also infuse a sense of responsibility for shrinkage in subordinate managers by holding them accountable for their annual shrinkage and by reflecting shrinkage results on annual performance reviews, which also triggers incentive bonuses. However, remember that if is difficult to hold anyone accountable for shrinkage levels in their area of responsibility if a company's inventories are sporadic or poorly conducted or if they have not been trained in loss prevention. Good, sound management that pays attention to detail and motivates employees can simultaneously increase sales while reducing losses.

Regional/District Operations Manager - In medium to large size retail chains, this individual implements corporate procedural and merchandising policies in the field, as well as supervises store managers. District managers influence the priorities of their store managers. For example, if clean floors and realigned display fixtures are stressed by the district manager during the store visit, these elements become the priority, sometimes at the expense of other operations. Therefore, district managers can help control shrinkage by continually stressing the need for loss prevention measures at the store level as well as supporting their counterparts (the loss control district managers) in their activities. District-level operations, and loss control and human resource representatives can form a triad by keeping each other informed of their activities and presenting an organized, unified front. This team approach helps to ensure that all company priorities are addressed and objectives are achieved.

Store Manager - Store managers set the tone of operation in their stores. Whatever store managers stress and praise becomes important to their employees. If an employee detects a price switch, for example, the manager should compliment the individual. Loss control specialists assigned to stores must work in concert with all store employees. The store manager and loss control specialist on duty should check in with each other periodically and compliment the actions of one another. Safety and security are at stake and those issues far outweigh any petty differences that may exist. Store managers are responsible for their stores and their actions should be respected. Similarly store managers should foster a mutual professional respect between loss prevention and store operations personnel as both of these sources play an important part in boosting company profitability.

Store managers often receive bonuses based on quarterly results of their efforts. Profitability and shrinkage figures should be part of the requirement to receive an incentive bonus. If the store has tremendous sales figures but horrendous shrinkage, the company may not be making a profit. The shrinkage goals that are set must be achievable and store managers must be able to incrementally reduce their shrinkage or the concept of reward has little value.

Store/Distribution Center Employees - While store detectives are the security department's first line of defense against shoplifting, store and distribution center employees are the company's first line of defense against theft and waste. As a group, store employees play the largest role of all in day-to-day control of losses. These individuals must be trained to recognize and report loss situations and rewarded by their supervisors.

Miscellaneous Company Employees - Regardless of the size of the corporation, all employees from buyers to corporate office staff should be made aware of loss threats that exist within their span of control and be told what they can do to deter these threats.

Store managers and their associates are the key to shoplifting control.

5
PROGRAMS AND PROCEDURES

This chapter highlights some programs retailers can implement as part of their loss control plan. As with personnel and systems approaches to loss control, programs must be selected on a priority basis and tailored to the specific needs of each retail organization.

Retailers should realize that their employees need direction and guidance. Standard operating procedures provide their managers, who are often isolated and thousands of miles from their supervisors, with a handy reference to guide their actions. The difference in having well-planned procedures versus being unprepared could impact the future of the business.

Programs designed to control losses can be categorized as policies, procedures, training and follow-up.

LOSS CONTROL POLICIES

Retailers should study loss control policies that have proven successful in other retail chains and design a similar policy based on the particular circumstances of their operation. These policies should have specific objectives, such as to control access, require supervisory verification of certain transactions, require that shoplifters be prosecuted, etc. A policy tells employees where the company stands on specific issues and what the company will do if the policy is disregarded. All policies should be fair, consistent, and documented. Assemble a policy manual and distribute copies to all stores and department heads. Review and update these policies periodically.

Examples of Recommended Policies

Non-disclosure of Proprietary Information - the information that is not to be disclosed to anyone, unless specifically authorized.

Conflict-of-Interest Statements - the company's positions on outside employment and business with vendors.

Alcohol and Substance Abuse - a policy for screening, detecting and treating employees with abuse problems.

Expense Accounts - accepted business expenses and established expenditure limits.

Contact with the Press - restrictions on making public statements regarding company activities.

Ethics - accepted and unaccepted ethical behavior.

Employee Pre-employment Screening - established criteria the applicant must meet prior to being hired by position.

Apprehension, Detention and Disposition of Dishonest Employees and Shoplifters - the company's stance on the detection and handling of theft suspects, including criminal prosecution, termination of employment, and civil action.

Evacuation of Premises - criteria that must be met prior to ordering an evacuation of the premises and those individuals authorized to order such actions.

Auditing Payables - importance of periodic audits of accounts payable activity.

LOSS CONTROL PROCEDURES

Security procedures build on the stated company policies by telling employees how to carry out the policies. Like policies, procedures should be researched and tested before implementation. They also should be included in the Operating Procedures Manual along with their corresponding policies. Some of the more common loss control procedures are discussed in the following pages.

Procedural Controls
Procedural controls for cash handling, merchandise handling, paperwork routing and safety are designed to limit risks by limiting access or vulnerability.

Merchandise controls reduce loss of merchandise at distribution centers and stores. Distribution center controls include separating receiving and shipping areas, verifying purchase orders, separating items, hanging items, EAS tagging, store distribution assignment, protective packaging, and shipping. Store controls include receiving, individual item or carton count variances, processing, display techniques, secure storage of high-loss or high-risk items, protection from elements, return-to-vendor procedures, damaged merchandise log-in and disposal, clerk check-out of merchandise or containers, and employee package checks.

Situational or Informations Procedures
These procedures provide guidance to employees at all levels and includes the following:

Shoplifting - This procedure dictates the criteria an employee needs to satisfy in order to detain a shoplifting suspect and explains the steps to follow in processing the case. To avoid costly lawsuits, this policy and procedure must be well-designed and employees should be thoroughly trained in following this procedure.

PROTECTION PROGRAMS

Programs designed to control losses are an extension of established policies and procedures. For the purpose of this book, programs are broken down into three categories based on the objective of the program - deterrence, detection and recovery.

Deterrence Programs

Deterrence programs are primarily designed to prevent theft by discouraging criminal activity, making theft incidents less probable, or by providing data used to plan future prevention programs.

New Store/Site Selection

The place to start when designing a loss control program is the site of a new store or other facility. Whether the new location is to be built from the ground up or remodeled from an existing structure, the security of company assets must be considered from the start of the planning cycle. Many factors are considered when new store sites are being evaluated and they include

- Demographics (i.e. number of target customers in the area)
- Visibility of the location
- Accessibility of the site
- "Anchor" or other stores in the same center if the site is located in malls or strip centers
- Available support services
- Expenses per square foot
- Available advertising support
- Area crime patterns

Crime potential is the primary concern of the loss prevention specialist when evaluating a new site. A security employee should conduct a survey of the area and gather input from other area merchants and law enforcement agencies regarding past and projected criminal activity in the proposed site area. The likelihood of crime in the area may not cause a particular site to be abandoned, but the information allows the company to plan and budget for appropriate security efforts.

Store Environmental Design

Just as stores are laid out to positively influence the customer's buying behavior, display fixtures and walls can be designed to discourage pilferage and theft by creating physical and psychological barriers, and surveillance opportunities.

The environmental design and physical layout of individual stores can impact the behavior of the retail shopper. Marein and co-workers noted,

> *"The retail store is a bundle of cues, messages and suggestions which communicate to shoppers. The retail store is not an exact parallel to the skinner box, but it does create mood, activate intentions, and generally affect customer reactions."*

Environmental cues that say "do not steal" or "buy this" are not necessarily mutually exclusive. Store planners can place interior walls and merchandise display fixtures in patterns that can accomplish the dual goals of increased merchandise visibility and protection. The goal of the environmental design concept is to minimize the opportunity to commit a crime in two ways. The first technique involves blocking access to specific areas or merchandise with physical barriers, such as cash registers, walls, display fixtures, locked doors, and merchandise tie-downs. Psychological barriers, such as "Employees Only" signs, also serve to discourage unauthorized personnel from entering into sensitive areas.

The second design technique, surveillance opportunity, opens up displays of high-risk merchandise to better observation by store employes and/or larger groups of customers. For example, by removing the large signs or 6-foot high merchandise fixtures from blocking the view of employees at POS locations, the chances of a potential shoplifter being spotted or deterred increase. Also, channeling the flow of customers near potential crime areas that have walkways is a form of a surveillance opportunity design technique. Other examples of crime control using environmental design include the following:

- Eliminate blind spots by rearranging racks or by installing CCTV, domes, or mirrors.

- Place high-risk merchandise displays near employee work areas and away from exits.
- Keep aisles containing tall merchandise fixtures straight and wide enough to allow full observation.
- Fit emergency exits with audible-sounding, observable, panic alarms to discourage shoplifters from using them as covert exit points.
- Limit the number of customer exits and entrances and control them by fire marshall approved turnstiles, protect them by EAS sensors, and monitor them by POS stations whenever possible.
- Install covert surveillance areas in walls, ceilings, or pillars where store personnel are able to survey the sales floor and use two-way mirrors, false air-conditioning vents and peepholes.
- Design receiving and stockroom areas to eliminate hiding places and provide clear observation of the work area to prevent dishonest activity.
- Ensure the exterior of the building and parking areas are well-lighted, fenced-off from potential problem areas (such as teen hang-outs, liquor stores, and bars), and readily observable from inside the store.

Control Procedures

As mentioned earlier, control procedures may be considered a program. This type of program may, in fact, be one of the least expensive, since there is generally no capital requirement. This format reinforces the fact that loss prevention should be practiced every day.

Employee Awareness

Develop a system, not a program

The message employees need to hear may change slightly, but the intended call to action remains consistent: Recognize and report causes of loss. In order to get the majority of company employees on the team, and keep them there, design the awareness activity as a system, not a program. (See figure 5-1)

The Focused Employee Awareness System

Step 1 - Identify/Prioritize Loss Risks

Objective(s): Identify company's major problems in order to better target prevention messages

1. Observe flow of money, merchandise and data through company
2. Interview employees and managers
3. Collect reported incidents
4. Analyze collected data for trends and indications
5. Prioritize identified risks

Step 2 - Develope Awareness Programs

Objective(s): Design plan for creating company awareness based on greatest need

1. Determine/select appropriate messages (ie. how to recognize, react to threat, utilize counter-measures, etc.)
2. Determine/select appropriate communication mediums (ie. videos, posters, etc.), and best presentation style
3. Pretest message mediums for acceptance and effectiveness
4. Identify tasks/personnel involved, **total** costs & timelines
5. Get program approved and funded

Step 3 - Train/Educate Employees

Objective(s): Teach employees to recognize, react to and report problems

1. Train all trainers to standard
2. Trainers consistently present information in the form of short, interactive workshops

Step 4 - Reinforce/Enhance Prevention Information

Objective(s): Expand and reinforce prevention messages and the company's commitment to prevention; compensate for continous employee turnover

1. "Stakeout" loss prevention centers in each store, office and distribution facility for bulletins and posters
2. Utilize paychecks, P.A. systems, brochures, short meetings to keep prevention messages visible

Step 5 - Encourage Desired Responses

Objective(s): Facilitate the call to action: refrain from and report deviance in the workplace; enhance **two-way** communication

1. 24 hour, toll-free, anonymous hot-lines deter & detect deviance
2. Place hotline number on wallet cards, refrigerator magnets, stickers, paychecks, posters, etc.
3. Advertise and encourage an in-person and/or in-writing open-door policy between management and associates

Step 6 - Recognize and Reward Desired Efforts

Objective(s): Motivate all employees to prevent and report problems year-round; loss control must **remain a priority**

1. Recognize employees for their good-faith efforts, not just based on outcome of cases
2. Newsletters, bulletin boards, name tag ribbons, store meetings allow high visibility recognition of teamplayers (except naming employees turning in dishonest co-workers)
3. Financially reward with cash, redeemable points etc. for performing desired actions

Step 7 - Review and Adjust Awareness Program

Objective(s): Review program focus, components, logistics, compliance and effectiveness for improvement

1. Grade communication messages and mediums for effect
2. Survey random employees and program personnel
3. Review reported incident changes, recovery totals and shrinkage results to help determine program impact

©1993 Read Hayes, CPP

(Figure 5-1)

Identify and prioritize loss risks

Many companies roll out their awareness campaign somewhere between steps 3 and 4 of our system. Mass produced, clip-art posters are slapped up in breakrooms, slogans are printed on coffee mugs and groups of employees "celebrate" their awareness of shrinkage in small meetings company-wide. All of these practices are acceptable, in fact recommended. However, the most important part of the program -step 1- is missing. Time, energy and expense can be more efficiently expended if the shrink reduction program is focused on the company's high priority problems initially. Every company, and every store or department within a company, has its own set of problems. The primary security decision maker in each company must take a step back and view the retail operation as a continuum. It is at this point that certain questions are posed: Where are we losing our cash, our information, our merchandise (assets to be protected)? Is most of it from the distribution center; in transport; from the stores (vulnerabilities)? Who's causing our losses: employees; customers; vendors (identify the threats)? How well is our current protection program working (state of current security)?

Observe and interview employees, review past incident reports and conduct audits. Areas of the company creating the most significant financial losses will be determined. As a general rule, approximately twenty percent of your stores, twenty percent of employees, twenty percent of the merchandise mix etc. will present eighty percent of corporate losses. The analysis of a thorough vulnerability survey should reveal high priority loss areas. These are the targets of our focused awareness system.

Put it together

The message to be delivered to targeted employees and how to best deliver it are the objectives of this phase. All employees must know how to recognize and report causes of loss. Printed material, video training kits, public address messages and employee meetings are examples of the mediums available

As the program is built and costed, delivery schedules and all involved personnel must be identified. Those involved may include non-security personnel such as managers as well as outside vendors if they are selected to help design and/or deliver at least part of the shortage control message. The key is to take the time to put together a total system and clearly identify what roles are to be played and when. Nobody should be surprised later by actual costs or the expectation of their personal involvement. Be realistic. Don't underestimate the amount of time and effort required to implement and manage an effective awareness program.

Commitment starts at the top

Senior management must be thoroughly briefed and involved. Nothing adds credibility to loss prevention awareness faster than a sincere plea from the CEO. Periodic interest on the part of these same executives throughout the year help keep it going. It is these same executives that must also approve the program's funding. They deserve a brief, but complete, explanation.

Spread the word

Most agree, employees must be given the message. What the message is was decided in Step 2. Now we must execute the training plan.

Interactive workshops of varying length are recommended. All attendees at these seminars should be encouraged to provide their thoughts and ask questions. Involvement insures greater retention and commitment. The duration of individual meetings may depend (and should) on the work flow in stores and distribution centers. Efficiency is today's business byword. Extra hours, taken away from normal duties, to attend workshops on any topic are rare, almost a luxury. Forty-five minutes is the average duration of most workshops. Due to short time frames, limit topics discussed (i.e. employee theft, safety, shoplifting detection and reaction, etc.) to one per meeting.

If possible, include 10 minute video presentations in each workshop given. The **professional** quality of videos tends to grab the attention of attendees. In order to hold their attention, videos should be fast-paced, well written and realistically acted. Bad or slow moving productions have minimal effect. They may even reduce company credibility if they're too bad!

Another very important component of this phase is consistency. All trainers should themselves be trained and then observed during a mock presentation. Remember, any workshop should educate and entertain. Good material poorly presented has limited impact. Good trainers increase the positive effect and ultimately the success of the program.

Repeat and reinforce

Employee awareness is or should be a self-perpetuating process. Training workshops should continue. Employee turnover is a fact of retail and requires extra effort to be considered the norm. Because sales events such as back-to-school, summer vacation and winter holidays drive store staffing levels, printed materials such as: posters, brochures, paycheck stuffers, etc. keep the loss prevention message before current employees. These messages include new and expanded information in addition to initial workshop material. The point is to insure that employees see (and understand) the security message. Remember, loss prevention is "competing" with messages from sales, operations and human resources, just to name a few.

Just as workshops and videos should clearly and professionally deliver information, so should reinforcement material. Make it look good. Presentation is a key to marketing to any medium.

Call to action

Understanding loss problems is important. So is understanding how to recognize problems. But the point is to get our target audience (employees) to act. Clean up spilled water that could cause a customer to fall, report an employee giving away merchandise to friends, or call for a price check when it appears a price sticker has been tampered with. If at least some of our employees are deterring potential losses, company-wide, consistently, we have won the battle. Shrinkage levels will come down.

This phase of the awareness system strives to elicit the desired response from employees (action or reaction). Some companies use hotlines, others mail-in cards. The goal is two-way communication. Employees talking to supervisors, up and down the chain of command. Data released from the National Retail Security Survey indicates most retailers now use some form of employee hotline for this reason.

Because a manager may become involved in inappropriate behavior or an employee wishing to report a major problem may have committed some "minor" policy violation (such as giving an unauthorized employee discount), some form of anonymous reporting should be provided. All employees must know how to access these reporting programs. Wallet cards, stickers, and posters give reporting instructions a high profile. High profile messages also work as a deterrent to the employee population as a whole. Anyone, at any given time, may exercise their concern and report a problem.

It's your job yes, but thanks

Corporate executives receive bonuses for achieving goals. Workers in countries struggling to cast off the yoke of communism never did. And shrinkage goals can be met if all employees make it a priority. The carrot and stick approach appears to be the best way to reach desired goals. The initial survey (Phase 1) focused the awareness program; the second phase saw the program developed; and steps three through five put it in motion. Phase six insures that people take it seriously. They will know the company is serious about loss reduction when goals are backed up with an appropriate reward. When employees are recognized for inspired efforts as well as results, they will continue to perform. Loss control must remain a priority. It doesn't take long before many programs begin to fizzle. Employees and security program managers tire of just being excited about loss prevention. To sustain program success, recognize and reward employees.

Store managers should acknowledge desired loss prevention behavior both directly to the involved employee, and to that employee's peers (one exception is the confidential reporting of deviance on the part of a fellow employee). Newsletters, store meetings and special ribbons for a name badge are all excellent ways to highlight team players publicly.

Reward can also take different forms. Some companies give cash awards or gift certificates. Both can by very expensive, but very effective. Several companies have decided NOT to give cash, gift certificates or their own store merchandise. If one employee was rewarded for acting to prevent loss and was given a substantial reward, another person who felt likewise entitled, yet slighted, may simply take something from the store to make up for it.

These companies use a system that allows them to issue bonus points. Employees can accumulate points during a calendar year that must be redeemed by March 31st of the following year. These points are applied to items in a prize catalog, much like a sales incentive program. A simple two-part form is completed by an authorized manager or loss prevention staff member. The number of points awarded is based on whether the employee assisted in a recovery, deterrence, or actual apprehension. The employee is issued a check for those bonus points which can be saved or redeemed at will. The average award totals just $7.00. For less than $10, these companies achieve as much impact as $100 in cash. However, any reward system is better than no reward system. Companies should look at a variety of reward options.

Again, the point is to keep the majority of employees on board. Watching, reacting and reporting problems. Keeping profit draining losses to a bare minimum.

Check it and fix it

Like any program, the focused awareness system should be periodically audited. Program managers and targeted employees should be asked for their perceptions. Are they more aware of loss causes and solutions now than before? Is the program operating as designed? Are problems being reported?

Also, reported incident trends, shrinkage levels and dollars recovered should be compared to previous years. Conclusions should not be jumped to! Any program needs to be given a chance. By the same token, just having a program, any program, is not the goal. Reduced loss is the goal. An annual objective review should clearly indicate where changes are best made.

Summary

Employee awareness programs are vital to reducing loss in any type of company. To be most effective, however, they should address the most significant problems first. To gain the most bang for the buck, the message and how it is presented should be clear and consistent. Professional programs, whether designed and presented in-house or partially or completely outsourced are financially possible for any company. Amateur productions are fine if they don't come off as such.

Public Awareness Campaigns

In many states, retailers band together to form retail associations to further their common interests. One program often promoted by these associations is a public awareness campaign aimed at making the negative result of a shoplifting arrest a high-visibility issue. Local law enforcement agencies also contribute to this effort by holding discussions with local groups, such as school children in all grades.

Shoplifter Education Programs

Many businesses and communities are utilizing shoplifter education programs. These courses are either self-study or group sessions that criminal court systems refer first time offenders to. By making shoplifters aware of the varied consequenses of their theft, these courses attempt to reduce the likelihood an offender will repeat their crime. Ongoing research is being conducted to determine the longterm effectiveness of diversion programs.

DETECTION PROGRAMS

Detection programs are implemented to detect theft, indications of theft, or vulnerabilities to theft. Prominent examples of this type of program include exception reports, auditing and store agent patrol.

Store Agent Patrol

By using plainclothes loss prevention specialists to supplement technology, retailers will detect shoplifters that previously went unnoticed. The use of store detectives is generally considered a reactive measure, but may actually be the ultimate form of deterrence, since it is difficult to steal while in the custody of store agents or police authorities. Any agents used by retailers should be carefully selected and thoroughly trained.

Recovery Program

Prevention of loss is the key to any loss control program, but the following programs allow retailers to recoup some of their losses. The following three programs are effective recovery programs.

Civil Action - When retailers fall victim to theft, they may take tort action against offenders in an attempt to recover lost assets in the form of damages. By using civil demand, retailers can help offset some of their losses and security costs.

Insurance - By adequately covering risk areas with insurance policies, retailers may be able to lessen the damage they sustain from theft and disaster.

Tax Write-Offs - State and federal tax laws allow deductions for many types of losses incurred by retail chains.

Fitting/Dressing Room Control

Many apparel retail stores have fitting/dressing rooms in their stores. These areas provide shoplifters with ideal locations to steal unless some type of control is established. Dressing room control procedures provide retailers with a tremendous opportunity to prevent thefts. A good dressing room control program should ensure that either an employee is assigned to the dressing room area on a full-time basis or that salespeople escort customers to the dressing rooms. Limit the amount of items permitted in a dressing room to eight per person. Provide the customer with a pre-numbered tag that correspond to the number of hangers being taken into the dressing room. The retailer may also use plastic tags that have a specific number of notches on them that correspond to the number of hangers being taken into the room. Control of these tags is very important. Keep a logbook or post a display board out of the customer's reach to track merchandise flow to and from specific dressing rooms. Be aware that shoplifters may steal #0, #1, or #2 tags for later use. A typical shoplifting scenario at a dressing room may be one in which the subject takes eight garments and a #8 tag into the room. Once inside the room, the subject conceals the #8 tag, hides seven items, and exits with one item and a #1 tag that was previously stolen.

Clerks assigned to the dressing room area can prevent losses while increasing sales. While checking customers into the dressing room, the clerk can make positive comments about the customer's taste in garments and can suggest additional sales. Smart managers put their best sales people in the dressing room area. Clerks in this area are often the first employee the public sees and this is the retailer's chance to make a good impression.

POLICY AND PROCEDURE MANUALS

As the number of lawsuits against retail firms continue to increase, retailers are looking for ways to better protect themselves against adverse rulings. One of the most effective ways to protect retailers is to have a written policy and procedure manual - policies and procedures regarding the prevention of theft and error are among the most important. Every company should have a policy manual and security procedures should be an entire section in this manual. Some retailers also prefer to have a separate loss prevention manual.

Regardless of the format used, important points to keep in mind include:
- Document procedures
- Update procedures periodically
- Adhere to procedures as closely as possible

While the establishment of sound procedures may greatly assist in defending a civil claim, these same procedures can cause the retailer to quickly lose the case if it can be shown they were not common knowledge or were not used in the field.

The policy and procedure manual is an integral part of any loss control program. The manual should reflect the policies of the organization and should detail how they are to be carried out. By implementing and following sound procedures, the retailer ensures a consistent, long-term approach to reducing losses.

TRAINING EMPLOYEES

After procedures have been designed, employees must be shown how to implement and use them. Orientation and training are the keys to successful accomplishment of profit goals. Training is one of the most neglected facets of any organization. It is either ignored, underfunded, or assigned to individuals that have no training experience. Employees at all levels must strive to achieve competence in their field and become aware of those habits that make them good or bad at their jobs.

A good trainer must be both competent and conscientious, and training sessions must be well-planned and lively. Each workshop should combine a little entertainment with a lot of education. The trainer must interact with the trainees to allow for a two-way flow of ideas and methods.

Loss prevention training takes two primary forms in any retail company - orientation and training on non-security employees, at all levels, in tasks they can perform to reduce losses, and training security employees on their specific duties. There are several well-produced training videos, with workbooks, available to retailers. These programs may be presented by company employees or outside experts.

To train loss prevention employees, retailers must put together a comprehensive in-house, or solicit an outside, training program. There are training schools available that provide retail security training. Retailers may hire graduates of these courses, have instructors come to the retailer's facility to train employees, or send their employees to the training institute's facilities.

Suggested courses for entry-level training include: retail theft laws; detection, surveillance and apprehension techniques; safety procedures; employee awareness training techniques; physical security; and report writing.

Training is the single most important factor in boosting productivity and reducing losses. It is also the least utilized technique. The realities of day-to-day business often force retailers to postpone or cut back training programs. As a result, the entire organization is weakened and may never achieve its goals.

FOLLOW-UP

Policies and procedures have been designed and implemented, and employees have been trained in their use. Now retailers must follow-up on these activities to ensure the success of their long-term loss control program. Follow-up occurs in three forms - testing and update, reward and recognition, and direction and discipline.

Testing and Updating Policies, Procedures and Programs

The retail industry is a rapidly changing industry. Because of this fact, no loss control program can remain completely relevant for very long. For example, a policy to control direct store delivery may become obsolete when vendors begin distribution center deliveries exclusively.

For these reasons, the retailer must periodically audit and alter procedures and programs currently in use. Some of the questions to ask about each policy, procedure or program include, Does this policy fit our corporate or department objectives? Does this procedure unnecessarily hinder the flow of business? Is there a better way? Is the program working? Is this procedure being used?

Recognition and Reward

Employees should be motivated by their leaders to follow procedures and prevent losses by having their supervisors recognize and reward their efforts. Employee meetings and get-togethers are the perfect forum for recognizing the contribution of a certain employee to the company's profitability. By calling control practices to the attention of employees, a retailer may reward one employee and deter another from dishonest activity at the same time.

A formal reward program is recommended to ensure that loss control remains a priority with employees. Employees are in a position to make a significant difference in a company's annual shrinkage figure and in today's society, the businessperson must use proven incentives to accomplish their objectives.

Direction and Discipline

Supervisors must give their employees specific direction, in the form of training, to perform their jobs adequately and to follow company procedures. If employees fail to follow a particular procedure, supervisors should gain control by applying discipline.

Discipline is defined as training or instruction that corrects, molds, or perfects actions and is exercised to imposed order and reasonable control. Supervisors must maintain some level of discipline in order to keep their groups focused and productive to accomplish corporate and department goals. All discipline should be applied in an objective and consistent manner.

6
SECURITY SYSTEMS AND PRODUCTS

Employees are the single most effective tool retailers have to reduce shoplifting losses. However, when retail companies reduce in-store staffing to a bare minimum, technology and products must fill the gap. Another key point, store staffs are steadily being reduced. Properly used, loss prevention technology may ultimately make the difference between high and low shrinkage in most companies if not all. Because most security systems can be capitalized, they are often times very affordable.

Physical security products help deter and detect shoplifting by placing physical and psychological barriers between all types of shoplifters and your lifeblood, store merchandise.

Any physical design should be based on an integrated approach. It should provide protection in depth, contain mutually supporting elements, and be coordinated to minimize gap or overlap in responsibilities and performance. An integrated system
- continuously analyzes existing protective measures.
- identifies possible interference with the operational capabilities of installations from any or all sources.
- carefully evaluates all measures that cost-effectively maintain security at the desired level.
- is tailored to the needs and local conditions of each location or activity.

Miscellaneous security systems

Merchandise alarms are hooked up to high-cost/high-loss merchandise (such as electronics). This alarm sounds when the circuit is broken by a shoplifter taking the protected item from its display case.

AS (Article Surveillance)

Article surveillance technologies serve to prevent theft activity by creating or elevating deterrence. There are currently two types of AS available (See figure 6-1). Electronic Detection Devices (or Electronic Article Surveillance) deter theft by increasing the certainty that attempted theft of tagged merchandise will be detected.

Usually when tagged merchandise passes the system's antenna, an audible alarm or announcement is sounded. To gain maximum benefit from electronic detection systems, the following steps are recommended:

1. Identify high-loss/risk merchandise.
2. Design and follow a tagging plan: include items to be tagged, by whom and how different types of merchandise are to be tagged.
3. Set up and follow a system test schedule. The equipment must work.
4. Implement an alarm response policy including who and how to respond, as well as incident documentation procedures.
5. An EAS/EDD training program for all of the above. This program must take into account constant turnover.
6. Audit and adjust your AS at least quarterly.

Benefit Denial Devices (BDD's) deter theft by increasing the certainty that merchandise an individual is attempting to steal will provide them with no benefit (i.e. personal use or resell value) since BDD's when tampered with, damage or destroy the protected merchandise

All tag detachers should be secured and numerically serialized to prevent or discourage their theft.

The following questions should be asked by any retailer investigating AS systems:

- What technology is used?
- What is the detection or pick rate?
- What is the false alarm rate and what causes it?
- What types of tags are available?
- How can the system be defeated?
- How close to the alarmed exit can tagged merchandise be placed?
- What are the total annual costs (e.g., installation, replacement tags, training, maintenance, warranties)?
- What is the system's reputation? - References (at least three)
- What are the applicable state laws regarding EAS alarm detection and detention?

(See figure 6-1)

The cost of AS systems can be expensive, but should prove effective. However, the effectiveness of AS systems diminishes as time goes by if store employees fail to tag articles or react to alarms or use other prevention methods. No technology can stand on its own. It must be supplemented with human surveillance and follow-up. In order for any AS system to prove cost-effective over the long-term, senior management and store management must endorse its use and ensure that it is properly used. Employees must be trained in AS system use and properly supervised to add credibility to the system. All targeted goods must be kept tagged and alarm situations must be responded to.

CCTV

More and more retailers are using CCTV to prevent, detect and document theft activity in their stores and distribution centers. In a back-up role, CCTV can verify fire, burglar and robbery alarms, or other access control systems.

CCTV can be installed outside to observe parking lots and alleys, or installed inside to watch high-loss or unauthorized areas. Camera installation can be temporary or permanent. Portable camera kits are used by retail investigators to respond to suspected theft activity. The carrying case may include a small color-chip camera,

(6-1) Article Surveillance Operating Characteristics

Characteristics	Electronic Detection Devices (EAS)			Benefit Denial Devices (BDD)		
	Microwave (High Frequency)	Radio Frequency (Low Frequency)	Electro Magnetic (Very Low Frequency)	Dye Ampule (non-electronic)	Mechanical Merchandise Destruction (non-fluid)	Electronic Disabling (being developed)
Merchandise Application	Soft Goods	Hard/Soft Goods	Hard Goods	Soft Goods	Hard Goods	Video Game Cartridges, etc.
False Alarm Rate	Very Low	Frequency Splitting RF Very Good	Very Low	N/A; Susceptible to Vandals	N/A	N/A
Detection or Rate	Good	Frequency Splitting; Excellent; RF Very Good	Excellent	N/A	N/A	N/A
Defeat Techniques	Cover with body or foil, Pressure on tag	Cover with foil, Pressure on tag	Sometimes cover with body or foil	Remove tag outside of store (very difficult)	Remove tag outside of store (very difficult)	N/A
Antennae Width at Exit	+20 Feet	+8 Feet	+2 Feet	N/A	N/A	N/A
Tag Application and Removal Speed	Fast	Soft Tag — Very Fast; Hard — Fast	Very Fast	Moderate	Moderate	By vendor N/A or Moderate by Retailer
Hard and Soft Tag Integration	Limited	Yes	Yes	Yes	Yes	Yes

©1993 Read Hayes, CPP

(Figure 6-1)

two or three types of lenses, a portable monitor for aiming the camera, power cords, tools, mounting brackets, and a time-lapse VCR. These covert surveillance kits allow the investigator to respond to a location where theft activity is taking place and quickly install the equipment to record specific unlawful activity. By using this portable equipment, the retailer may avoid the investment of equipping an entire store. Smoked-glass panels or an Opti-Dome may be permanently installed and a camera may be swiftly installed when needed. Aim infrared sensors via lens' to detect movement. Movement triggers the VCR to turn on and the VCR records the target area.

Prominent display of the camera or dome is important to achieving deterrence. A sign, feedback monitor or flashing red diode are examples of highlighting techniques.

When placing CCTV cameras in stores in an attempt to deter crime, it is important to realize that the pervasiveness of simulated CCTV cameras has negated their deterrent effect to some extent.

Cameras can be equipped with a variety of lenses including zoom, split-image, night vision, covert (pin hole), right angle, and fixed focal length. The lens' used depends on the area or spot to be monitored, the distance to the target and the environmental conditions.

Time-lapse VCRs allow the retailer to record a full day's activity on the tape. If a dishonest act is believed to have occurred, the investigator can quickly review the tape. It is possible to produce instant still photos from CCTV video with an attachment.

Date/time generators (DTG) display the current date and time on the screen and can be used as evidence in criminal or civil trial proceedings. Some systems also display transaction data and can be programmed to record transactions of certain types or rung by selected employees.

The following questions should be asked when selecting and installing a CCTV system:

- Is a color or black-and-white television required?
- What type of lens is required?
- What type of VCR is needed?

- What type and size of monitor is desired?
- How should the camera be mounted and where?
- What will the light level be during the surveillance?
- Who will monitor the system and how often? What will my labor cost be?
- How will suspicious incidents be responded to?

Article Security

Article surveillance deters theft by increasing the certainty of detection, with little or no increase in employee labor intensity. Article security reduces loss by restricting unauthorized access to high-risk merchandise. This restriction inconveniences customers but may be required due to high losses, poor display visibility and/ or inability to afford article surveillance technology.

Secure merchandise displays and tie-downs - High risk merchandise, such as jewelry or handguns, should be kept in secure display cases. High-risk apparel, such as fur coats, leather jackets and men's suits, should be kept on display fixtures that require a clerk to access them. While this can be very inconvenient, it should save a tremendous amount of merchandise from unauthorized removal. Also, high-loss electronics and luggage can be tied down with metal cables to discourage easy grab-and-run thefts.

Other loss prevention systems - A combination of Article surveillance and article security involves oversized plastic cassette tape cases or apparel tags which include EAS tags designed to alarm when tampered with.

Bar coding - Bar coding allows a retailer to quickly receive, distribute, and ring-up merchandise. This technology makes price-switching and under-ringing more difficult and can be combined with other technologies, such as inventory trackers, price look-up and EAS systems.

Subliminal messaging systems - As advertised by their manufacturers, subliminal messaging systems allow a retailer to broadcast messages (about working safely, staying honest, and being a hard worker) to employees through their music system. These systems present a message to individuals on a level below their conscious awareness. Examples of subliminal messages include, "Be friendly-greet every customer," "Accuracy is important," "Hard work leads to success," and "I am an honest person." Systems now available are virtually tamper-proof and the volume of the message adjust to the ambient sound level of the store or distribution center. It is recommended that retailers considering these systems thoroughly check state or local laws that may regulate the use of subliminal messages. **Also,** check all references and available scientific research data to confirm effectiveness.

Lighting systems - Designed to highlight merchandise the retailer wants featured, lighting systems can also be used to discourage shoplifting by overilluminating areas a shoplifter would normally use as a concealment area.

Colored signs - Since the beginning of time, different colors have symbolized different meanings. Red and black denote authority or signal the unknown. According to researchers Farrell and Ferrara, an example of the use of colors to discourage shoplifting is the placement of a stop sign in a high-loss area.

Researchers Farrell and Ferrara, in their book, *Shoplifting: The Anti-Shoplifting Guidebook*, suggest some of the following techniques to discourage shoplifting and employee theft:

- Distribute anti-theft pamphlets in the store or mall.
- Paint or display an eye or poster of an individual looking at customers to psychologically deter theft.
- Use intermittent, low sounds to put the potential shoplifter off balance.
- Display "Thou Shall Not Steal" buttons or stickers at point-of-purchase areas for sale.
- Display album covers of the rock group Police.
- Display a book with the word shoplifter in the title or display a bible.

Visual deterrents - Some retailers find that in some instances, displaying likenesses of police officers or security agents tend to discourage shoplifting activity. Life-sized cardboard cutouts or holographic projections are two methods used to display these images. This practice is intended to remind potential shoplifters of the consequences of theft. Be alert to complaints by honest customers. In some cases, these cutouts are actually stolen for souvenirs.

Identification dye sprays and marking pens - Use inks that are normally invisible, but illuminate under ultraviolet or "black" lights to mark merchandise or documents as belonging to a specific owner.

Surveillance aids (mirrors and observation towers) - Surveillance aids increase the retailer's ability to survey the sales floor for shoplifters. Mirrors can assist an employee in viewing merchandise or aisles, but may also be used by the shoplifter to look for employees. Many retailers build observation towers in storage rooms, which enable store agents to observe sections of the sales floor from concealed positions. The observation opening may be an air conditioning vent or one-way mirror. These towers can increase the shoplifting detection rate, but the agent temporarily loses sight of the perpetrator while climbing out of the tower and "bad stops" may result. Towers are best used (as is CCTV) with two agents who operate with 2-way portable radios to avoid loss-of-sight incidents. Also, many true professional shoplifters realize observation towers and mirrors are seldom used.

Counterfeit Refunds

More and more shoplifters are using insurance quote machines and personal computers to duplicate receipts. By counterfeiting receipts, they are able to return stolen merchandise for refund or claim unpaid-for merchandise at Customer Pick-Up areas. Multicolored POS ribbon with non-reproducible blue ink and custom ink color mixes allow receipts to be printed that are virtually impossible to counterfeit.

7

HANDLING THE SHOPLIFTER

For the purposes of this book, the handling of shoplifters has been broken down into seven steps. (See figure 7-1) It is important to understand how to properly spot shoplifters and take proper action. Prevention of theft is the key to reducing annual losses. The proper handling of shoplifters is actually a form of prevention. Albeit the least desirable. But no prevention program is 100% effective and, in fact, most may only be around 60% effective at best. Shoplifters of all types must realize that your company is serious about controlling the problem. The next seven steps should provide state of the art information on the various options available. Also keep in mind the potential for violence as well as the civil liability involved in mishandling a case of customer theft.

Step 1 - Detection of possible shoplifters
This is where it all begins. Regardless of the retailer's individual policies condoning the detention of suspected shoplifters or not, all store employees should understand how to spot shoplifters.
Behavioral Cues - Most individuals, when committing a dishonest act such as stealing, are under stress. They also must take possession of the desired item and then carry, conceal, consume or wear the item. All the while, they are probably watching for

Handling the Shoplifter: A Phased Approach

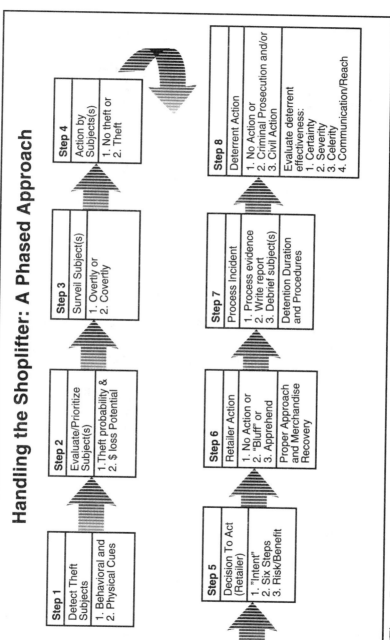

Step 1

Detect Theft Subjects

1. Behavioral and
2. Physical Cues

Step 2

Evaluate/Prioritize Subject(s)

1. Theft probability &
2. $ loss Potential

Step 3

Surveil Subject(s)

1. Overtly or
2. Covertly

Step 4

Action by Subjects(s)

1. No theft or
2. Theft

Step 5

Decision To Act (Retailer)

1. "Intent"
2. Six Steps
3. Risk/Benefit

Step 6

Retailer Action

1. No Action or
2. "Bluff" or
3. Apprehend

Proper Approach and Merchandise Recovery

Step 7

Process Incident

1. Process evidence
2. Write report
3. Debrief subject(s)

Detention Duration and Procedures

Step 8

Deterrent Action

1. No Action or
2. Criminal Prosecution and/or
3. Civil Action

Evaluate deterrent effectiveness:
1. Certainty
2. Severity
3. Celerity
4. Communication/Reach

©1993 Read Hayes, CPP

(Figure 7-1)

individuals that may try to stop them. It is because of these facts that all types of shoplifters may be detected by noting their behavior and how it is usually different from that of the honest customer. I have divided these behavioral cues into actions and reactions. Actions may indicate a person is about to steal, is currently stealing or has recently stolen.

Actions:
- Most customers hold merchandise up with their hands and look it over. They are noting the style or look of the item, its price and the quality. Shoplifters generally spend much more time looking for store employees or security. This is called "scoping".
- Also, a shoplifter's hands are usually down concealing or tampering with the merchandise, not up examining it.

Look for individuals that:
- Remain in corners, especially where they are hidden from view by displays.
- Have "phony" or whispered conversations with a companion.
- Seem nervous, turn red, light a cigarette, or constantly glance about, watching salespeople and customers.
- Move quickly around the store.
- Look at merchandise, replace it, then begin pacing and scoping.
- Refuse sales help and avoid salespeople and other customers.
- Avoid the front of the store and stay along the back of the store.
- Select merchandise quickly, without carefully choosing what they want.
- Move merchandise to the back of the store or to a more concealed display rack.

These are just a few examples of actions that may indicate dishonest activity.

Reactions:
Because most shoplifters are under tremendous stress throughout their theft sequence, they generally react in a more pronounced way to certain outside stimuli. Examples include, jumpiness, run-

ning, ditching or throwing merchandise down or walking hurriedly to a "blind" area such as a restroom, fitting room or behind tall racks. These overreactions usually result from an employee suddenly asking them a question, a police siren sounding outside or a P.A. announcement requesting "security to XYZ department", etc. The point is, dishonesty breeds anxiety. This nervousness is exhibited differently by different people, but most people under this amount of stress react more demonstrably than honest customers.

Physical cues - Another recommended way to spot potential shoplifters is by noting two types of physical cues. The first thing to look for is something that would indicate the capability for removing a quantity of merchandise. Empty bags inside a pocket or another bag, a large (open) purse, bag or bookbag, bulges around the lower part of the shirt or blouse possibly indicating a booster girdle, baggy pants which would allow concealment in elastic hose or socks are all examples of capability characteristics to be alert for.

The second physical tip-off of a potential shoplifter is known as the non-typical customer profile. The type and location of a store generally dictates the "look" of the average customer. Be aware, however, that there is no such thing as a true average customer, but an individual wearing inappropriate dress such as a raincoat in dry weather, etc. may also signal behaviorally their intent to steal. Most shoplifters are best detected by a combination of behavioral and physical cues.

Step 2 - *Evaluate and prioritize the situation and subjects*

Once a potential shoplifter has been spotted, a trained manager or loss prevention specialist should take over. If a theft takes place, it must be observed by a manager or specialist if an apprehension is to be attempted. The manager must determine if a suspected shoplifter merits further watching. Retail is a very demanding occupation and any task such as surveilling a possible shoplifter means something else is left undone. Also, there may be more than one suspected individual. The manager or specialist must quickly evaluate the situation. Determining the probability that a certain individual may steal is subjective, but behavioral and physical cues combined with the recollection of theft losses at that store are part of the equation. Another element that should be considered at this point is the financial loss potential of a particular incident. If there are two separate individuals that appear inclined to steal, all things being equal, the one eyeing the most expensive items is the one to stick with.

Step 3 - Surveillance of the subject(s)

The first rule of watching anyone you feel might steal: Watch their hands! Always watch their hands. With very, very few exceptions, people use their hands to take your merchandise.

Overt Observation - The next decision to make is if the observation should be conducted openly or surreptitiously. If the goal is apprehension, you must normally watch the individual steal and attempt to exit without their knowledge. If you'd prefer they know you're watching them in the hopes they'll leave without stealing your goods, the key is to continually let them know where you are and that you're watching. Also, let them know that you have a way of signalling your observation to others. This is called good "customer service." It is the best way to prevent theft. Any employee can do it. The suspect(s) should not however feel overly threatened or be intentionally and publicly embarrassed. If you are asked: "Are you watching me?" either don't reply or simply state: "Why, should I?" in a non-confrontational tone. The goal is prevention.

Covert Observation - The covert surveillance of subjects from the sales floor is perhaps the most difficult of all the techniques available. The agent must continually watch the suspect(s) without the primary suspect(s) or their accomplices spotting them. Some agents are able to look and act like an ordinary customer while observing the suspect from close range. Others prefer to observe from farther distances. In this case, they must parallel the subjects moves, always keeping the suspect's hands in view. Sometimes the agent will hide in merchandise fixtures. Another key is to stay low and still. Most shoplifters don't seem to look low. The human eye is also very sensitive to spotting movement. Some store agents use hand mirrors and small binoculars to look around corners or down long rows. Every company has tactics and techniques they may share with you. Also, there are loss prevention training courses available.

Step 4 - Subject's actions

This step highlights the actions taken by the subject(s) you have under surveillance. Do they steal or simply exit the store without stealing? If the subject leaves without committing a crime, the individual's face and vehicle should be committed to memory. If you feel certain that they were going to steal but changed their mind for whatever reason, let others know and keep an eye out for that individual in the future.

If the subject takes possession of your merchandise look to Step 5 for the next move.

Step 5 - Decision to Act

Once a shoplifter takes merchandise the retailer has three options:

No Action - The potential for violence, lack of trained store personnel etc. may dictate that the suspected shoplifter be allowed to leave with no action taken on your part. If this is the case, a short report should still be filled out and retained to document suspicious activity.

Burn or Recovery - In some situations, a retailer may not desire or be able to stop a suspected shoplifter. In this case, you may want to attempt a recovery. This procedure is discussed in Step 6.

Apprehension - The goals of detaining a person suspected of theft are to recover merchandise, identify the subject(s), debrief the subjects to learn their motivations and methods, and to process them (criminal and civil sanctions) for deterrence reasons.

Risk/Benefit

Before deciding on the proper course of action, you should quickly weigh the risk to benefit ratio of each option. No-action, eliminates the risk of injury or civil suit but fails to retrieve the merchandise or provide any form of deterrence. A burn may result in merchandise recovery and some temporary deterrence, but most burns or bluffs are unsuccessful. Also, the burn should not lead to a confrontation. An apprehension will normally lead to a recovery and some deterrence, but may be violent or if mishandled, could lead to civil litigation.

Six steps to success

The first key is "witness a theft", a basic rule of thumb must be: If you didn't see it, it didn't happen. In order to take any action at all, a member of management or a trained loss prevention specialist should have personally observed the actual theft. In the 1990's every retailer wears a large bull's-eye on their back. In other words, if any person, employee or customer, is falsely accused of theft, the retailer may be held civilly liable for their actions. Additionally, violent shoplifting incidents are increasing dramatically as drug abusers use retail stores as a convenient source of ready cash.

The decision to detain a shoplifting suspect should be based on sound company policy, but here are six steps we recommend following before you or your employees take action.

1. See the customer approach the item in question. This eliminates a later claim that the item belonged to them previously.
2. See the actual selection of the article.
3. See where the article is placed or concealed.
4. Keep the subject(s) under constant surveillance. If the individual drops the item, don't stop them. Just make a recovery and report.
5. Let the subject pass the last point of sale, without paying, before stopping them, if at all possible. This makes it difficult for them to claim they intended to pay for the merchandise.
6. Know where the articles are concealed on the suspect when making the stop. Tell the individual in a calm, professional manner that you are aware of the situation and in control.

Notice the first three rules all start with the word see. Remember that good customer service is the best deterrent to shoplifting. Most shoplifters will not attempt to steal if you're watching them.

Step 6 - Action by the retailer: Bluff/Detain

In step 5 the course of action was determined. Bluff or Detain is the normal choice.

Bluff/Burn

Most retailers are advised to attempt to get suspects to drop the goods before they leave the premises, rather than attempt an apprehension. There are several ways to recover merchandise, but remember that customers should never be accused of stealing. Retailers should attempt to "intimidate" subjects enough so that they will "ditch" the merchandise. Shoplifters normally avoid eye contact and don't like salespeople waiting on them or working around them. By looking directly and frequently at the subject, while "working" in close proximity, the subject may go and dump the shoplifted items if they're given a little space. Another method to get the suspects to drop the merchandise is to confront them without making accusations. Ask "helpful" questions such as, "Can I help you find a shirt to go with those pants?" This confrontation may make the shoplifter nervous. Continue making eye contact and stay close, but give the subjects enough room to ditch their merchandise.

If the shoplifter attempts to leave the store before the first two "bluff" techniques can be employed, a manager should walk quickly and loudly behind the subjects as they approach the exit. Many shoplifters will detour back into the store and dump the merchandise. If you wish to burn the suspects at this point, "startle" the suspects before they are so close to the exit, they are psychologically committed to exiting the store. Many shoplifters would rather risk apprehension than be too obvious in returning to the store. If a shoplifter confronts a store employee, the employee is best advised not to escalate the situation by arguing with a suspect. If all six steps have not been followed, the subject should be allowed to move on.

The point of these different techniques is to signal to suspects that a store employee is aware of their activity and is ready to take action. The retailer's ultimate goal is to recover merchandise without accusing a customer of theft.

Retailers should realize that while burns or bluffs sometimes work, they are temporary measures, since many shoplifters return to a store to steal again. This is especially true in the case of some professionals who often steal merchandise in order to obtain cash for illegal drugs.

Apprehending the shoplifter (consult your attorney on these points)

If the decision is made to apprehend a shoplifter (and all six steps have been followed), the manager or security specialist may wish to use some of the following suggestions: (See figure 7-2)

Wait until the suspect passes the last point of sale with the stolen merchandise. While not a requirement in many jurisdictions, this action helps to prove the suspect's **intent to steal the merchandise** in question. When possible, a second person should accompany the security specialist making the stop and act as a witness and back-up.

Move quickly behind suspects, then step in front of them to impede their direction of travel. Do not stand flat-footed and remain alert to attack or escape. Keep your hands free. Do not touch the suspect. If a suspect attempts to strike you or attempts to escape, use reasonable force to either defend yourself or detain the suspect. Consult your attorney on these points. It is never wise to pursue shoplifters for safety reasons.

Identify yourself by saying "I am a [manager/security specialist] for [company name]. I'd like to talk to you inside the store. Please come with me." At times, suspects may ask why you want them to return to the store. Without making an accusation, simply say, "I want to talk to you about some merchandise that may not have been paid for." Never suggest that the suspect "forgot" to pay for the items; this may be used as a defense in court. Don't get into an argument or discussion with suspects at this time. Encourage them to return to the store by saying that you'll discuss everything in the office. This is a good method to recover stolen merchandise in a low-key manner. Stay in charge. Do not show uncertainty.

Remember the first words of the suspect, especially if they resemble a "confession." Often, a suspect will say, "Can I just pay for it?" This is your assurance that the suspect has the item and may cooperate.

Escort suspects back into the store to a back room or office -

some place that provides some privacy. Observe their hands at all times to be certain that they do not dump the items prior to entering the office or pull some kind of weapon. Some companies have suspects carry their own packages. This will impede their actions and leave you free to deal with any situations that are created.

Keep the subject off balance mentally by continually asking them questions such as "How did you get to this store?" If a suspect asks, "What is going to happen to me?" just answer, "Let's talk about it." Don't give them a reason to attempt an attack or escape. Also, covertly signal a prearranged sign to another employee indicating they should notify law enforcement and store management. Remember, a shoplifter may immediately sense uncertainty and may exploit it to their advantage.

Step 7 - Processing the incident

Regardless of the action taken in a suspected shoplifting incident, a report should be filled out. All incidents should be documented.

Detaining the shoplifter

After the subject has been apprehended, the security specialist must handle the situation in a professional manner. Many states have statutes that allow merchants to detain shoplifting suspects based on probable cause (without making a formal arrest). This is in order to conduct an investigation to determine if the suspect either took store merchandise without permission or had the intent to steal. Detention and investigation must be conducted in a reasonable manner, for a reasonable length of time, without using excessive force or threats of prosecution to coerce a civil release or confession. If the security specialists determines that a theft took place, they may decide to take criminal and civil action.

Retailers may choose to follow some of the following guidelines when detaining a suspect: (See figure 7-2 and 7-3)

Once inside the private office, ask the suspects if they know why they have been asked to return to the store. This opens the door for a confession and keeps you from making any accusations.

If the suspects deny knowing why they were asked to return,

Shoplifting Apprehension

- Prevent rather than apprehend whenever possible!
- Only management or loss prevention can stop a shoplifter.
- Before stopping anyone, be able to answer...
  1. What is the item?
  2. Where is the item?
  3. Is the item still there?
  4. Have I followed all 6 steps?
  5. Do I have backup?
- **IF YOU DIDN'T SEE IT, IT DIDN'T HAPPEN!**
(Do not take a customer or employee's word that someone stole.
Use prevention techniques to get person "to dump" merchandise.)
- Give person every chance to pay for the items.
- Person can be stopped in an aisle only if package was opened, contents were concealed, and empty box was discarded.

Wallet Card - Side 1

Approach

1. Wait till person is past point of sale.
2. Always have a witness.
3. Identify yourself.
4. Ask person to speak with you a moment.
5. Have person hand you the items ASAP.
6. Escort person to private area of store.
7. If person refuses to come in store, **DON'T FIGHT!**
   Try to get items, obtain car tag # and description; **CALL POLICE.**
   - Fill out incident report.
   - If you decide to prosecute, call police immediately.
   - If you don't want to prosecute, **ask** person to sign form.
   - Juveniles can only be released to parents/guardians or police.
NO EXCEPTIONS! Have parent/guardian sign incident report.

Wallet Card - Side 2

(Figure 7-2 and 7-3)

(7-4) Sample Incident Report

Store Name: _____ Store Number: _____

Manager/Employee Name: _____

Date: _____ Time of Occurence: am/pm _____

Offense (Check One): Shoplift __ Employee __ Other (explain) _____
_____

Subject Name: _____

Subject Address (Street, City, State, Zip): _____
_____

Subject Phone ( ) - Race _____ Sex: _____ Age: _____

Hgt _____ Wgt _____ Hair _____ Eyes _____ SS# _____

Parent/Guardian Name(s): _____

Parent/Guardian Address: _____
_____

Explain Inciden in Detail (Who, What, Where, When) *include if merchandise was recovered, damaged saleable, lost, etc. _____
_____
_____ (con'd on back if necessary)

Juvenile _____ Adult _____ Arrested _____ Notice Form Issued _____

Evidence: Taken by Police _____ Held at Store _____ Other _____

Qty	Article Name/Description	Price
___		
___		
___		
___		
___		
___		

The listed articles have a total value of: $ _____
_____
_____

(Figure 7-4)

ask if there is an item that has not been purchased. If the suspects still deny everything, be more specific. Name the exact item and the location of concealment, and ask for the item. Remain calm but firm.

Once the merchandise has been recovered, analyze the suspect. Remove anything that could be used as a weapon (e.g., scissors, a pencil, etc.) from within reach of the suspect. For your protection, you generally have the right to search for weapons (females search females). If the suspect is uncooperative, call the police immediately and have them take over the situation. Local police or sheriff's departments can be contacted to demonstrate proper safety search techniques.

If the suspect is cooperative and you feel safe, begin filling out the incident paper work. Figure 7-4 is an example of a security incident report. Note that most police agencies prefer to have all paper work completed prior to their arrival. Any security/safety incident that takes place on company property should be documented and saved for at least three years. Incident reports serve as valuable evidence at subsequent criminal or civil trials. They are also very useful for incident projection. By tracking incidents by type, time and location, trends may become apparent - thereby allowing for better allocation of loss control resources.

It is not required that a non-law enforcement security agent read any "rights" to the suspect.

Never leave any detainee alone.

Question the shoplifter to recover all merchandise and determine identities of all suspects.

Obtain a confession and pick up any valuable intelligence or information the suspect may have about shoplifting activity in the local area. The practice of interviewing subjects that have been apprehended for shoplifting provides retailers with valuable information when planning loss prevention efforts. Note that many shoplifting suspects will refuse to talk, but those that do often provide information regarding the perception, "on the street," of security at various retailers in the surrounding area. Any information gained by the interviewer should be verified, if possible, by another source before being considered absolutely credible.

Ask suspects for a form of identification. Then ask suspects to state their full name, date of birth, and current mailing address. Compare the verbal information with the information printed on the subject's driver's license or other valid identification.

The *National Retail Theft Trends Report* bears out the belief that shoplifting tends to mirror customer profiles and peak shopping periods. Each retail company, however, should track certain data in order to study recorded incidents for trends. (See figure 7-5)

When the paper work is nearly finished, call the police if they haven't already been contacted if you decide to prosecute (from another room, whenever possible).

Don't make any threats or promises to the suspect, at any time.

If the subject is to be prosecuted, give the responding police officer the original report. Send a copy to the corporate offices, if applicable, and keep a copy in a locked file cabinet at the store. Record the case number, the name of the company employee who made the apprehension, and the police officer's name on the incident report.

Only detain the suspect for a reasonable length of time (1 hour is the average).

Grant any *reasonable* requests such as certain medications, bathroom privileges, or a drink of water. Use caution when granting requests for medication and trips to the restroom. If suspects say they are ill or need assistance of any kind, provide it immediately. Don't assume that it's a phony complaint. Remain alert for escape attempts.

After the police officer arrives, mark the evidence and seal it in a bag. Staple a copy of the incident report to the outside of the bag. Place the evidence in a locker (access to this locker must be limited to management and security) and do not disturb it until it is requested in court. Some states, or jurisdictions within states, allow retailers to photograph merchandise and require only a photograph during trial, thereby allowing the merchandise to be sold. A check with local prosecuting attorneys will provide the proper procedure to follow.

If a customer is detained in error, not only is this an awkward and embarrassing situation, but it could lead to legal action by the angry customer. Security specialists and other store employees can take the following steps to avoid liability claims.

Make an apologetic statement such as "Thank you for your

Retail Company _____ Store/DC. # ____ Case # _____

INCIDENT DATA

Type   ___01 shoplift   ___04 burglary
             ___02 dishonest employee   ___05 robbery
             ___03 vendor fraud   ___06 other_____

Time of Incident _____ a.m./p.m. **Date**___/___/___

Method Detected ___01 employee ___A security ___B non-security
                    ___02 customer
                    ___03 EAS
                    ___04 camera system
                    ___05 exception report
                    ___06 audit/inventory

Violence ___01 yes ___02 no **Weapon Used** ___01 yes ___02 no

Injury ___01 yes ___02 no

Subject under Influence ___01 yes ___02 no

Method of Theft (SH)	**Method of Theft (DE)**
___01 purse	___01 cash theft/no sale
___02 bag	___02 void fraud
___03 pocket	___03 merchandise theft
___04 clothing	___04 refund fraud
___05 price switching	___05 underring/discount
___06 grab/run	___06 failure to record sale
___07 consume	
___08 refund fraud	

SUBJECT DATA - # of offenders_____ (one report per offender)

Age___ ___01 adult ___02 juvenile **Sex** ___01 male ___02 female

Race ___01 white ___03 Hispanic ___05 native American
         ___02 Asian ___04 black   ___06 other _____

Offender Type ___01 amateur ___02 professional

Stated Motive for Theft ___01 desire item(s)
                             ___02 return for cash
                             ___03 purchase drugs
                             ___04 peer pressure
                             ___05 basic need item(s)
                             ___06 don't know why

MERCHANDISE TAKEN

Number of items taken_____   Amount $_____

©1993 Read Hayes, CPP

(Figure 7-5)

time; we apologize for any inconvenience you've experienced."

Be sincere. Stay calm. Be friendly, helpful and courteous.

If a customer appears hostile, antagonistic or outraged, politely excuse yourself and withdraw from the scene immediately. Indicate to the customer that you will summon the store manager.

Make absolutely no commitment to the customer, and above all, never admit liability.

Discuss the incident with no one except the Director of the Loss Prevention Department, the Director of the store, the Risk Management Department, representatives of the company's insurance brokers, and the company's insurance carriers and law firm.

If an immediate response is needed by the customer, get the store manager and have her inform the detainee that someone from the central office will contact him as soon as possible.

If possible, politely obtain the name and address of the customer. Do not insist. Obtain reports from employee witnesses and forward all documentation to the Risk Management Department as soon as possible.

Civil Action

If it is decided to pursue civil action under the more than 44 state civil demand statutes, the following guidelines are suggested. (See figure 7-6)

Fill out a report to take civil action against the person who was detained and only when the security specialist can prove that the subject did take cash or merchandise without proper permission and that the subject intended to deprive the company of the full value of the cash or merchandise.

Avoid civil action against individuals who may be unable to form criminal intent, such as juveniles under the age of 10, and aged/elderly persons or those under the care of a physician for emotional disorders.

Make every attempt to properly identify the subjects that committed the theft. Ask for two forms of identification. If the suspect is a juvenile, get both parents' names.

Obtain a current mailing address, including city and zip code, and a current phone number.

Criminal and Civil Process

CRIME
Criminal wrong against the state

TORT
Civil wrong against a person or corporation

THEFT ACT (Crime/Tort)

APPREHENSION

ACTION (By Retailer)

May pursue both

Criminal side:

STATE ACTION (Criminal)

CRIMINAL PROSECUTION

(Loss of Freedom)

INCARCERATION or PROBATION

&/or

RESTITUTION

(May cover cost of merchandise lost and not cost of prosecution for retailer)

&/or

FINE

A. Punitive
B. Court Costs

Civil side:

TORT ACTION (Civil)

CIVIL DEMAND

DAMAGES

1. **ACTUAL DAMAGES**
   A) General — cost of pursuit of theft (Security costs)
   B) Special — cost of loss to company (not necessarily merchandise)
2. **PUNITIVE** — To deter wrongful action.

©1993 Read Hayes, CPP

(Figure 7-6)

Avoid the appearance of extortion by not accepting payments at the point of apprehension or by threatening subjects with criminal prosecution if they fail to satisfy your demands.

Ensure that the incident report includes full name, driver's license number or state-issued identification number, current and complete mailing address, and a short narrative describing the incident.

Send a legible copy of the incident report to the civil recovery firm or to other appropriate individuals or groups.

Positively identify theft suspects

A person apprehended for theft can usually be prosecuted criminally, asked or sentenced to provide restitution and civilly demanded simultaneously.

Retailers are advised to consult with their attorney for specifics, but the recovery process is relatively simple.

To collect the damages under this law, a business can either use an outside firm (the national trend due to the time and expense of setting up an in-house program) to handle the process or designate a person within the company to initiate and follow-up on all cases. Typically, a theft suspect is detained and a short written report is made by the merchant. Every attempt should be made to obtain a correct current mailing address either from the subject himself or through the police. All reports must be reviewed for completeness and to confirm that the case satisfies elements required to prove that the detained subject in fact committed theft. Next, the case is entered into a computer and a letter of demand referring to the incident and state statue is sent to the subject. Also included is a copy of the appropriate state law and the name and phone number of the company's contact person. If no response is received within a specified time, a second letter is sent. Most civil demand service companies charge a small fee of 25-30% of any money collected by the company. This fee covers collecting and screening all reports, letter services and tracking all incidents that occur. They also provide sample report forms to smaller companies. The attorney involved continually tracks all applicable state laws and deals with attorneys or governmental agencies for the retailer. In most states a structured payment plan can be set up with subjects in order to make recovery easier.

Also, many states allow a parent or guardian to be held civilly liable for their juvenile's actions. By holding the parent financially accountable for their dependant's actions, closer supervision is the anticipated eventual outcome. Closer supervision may have a positive impact on many of today's problems, including drug abuse and school dropouts which all increase shoplifting losses.

Civil action for theft

When a customer or employee steals from a company, that action is both a crime and a civil tort. (See figure 7-5)

In both cases, a third party with a legal expertise is generally utilized. In the case of criminal action, the state or district attorney must file an information or secure an indictment to prosecute the offender.

The following information explains some of the differences between criminal action and civil (tort) action and references the attached chart.

BURDEN OF PROOF - "What is required to get a conviction or judgement?"

CRIMINAL ACTION - The state must prove beyond any reasonable doubt the individual is guilty. This is sometimes difficult to prove.

CIVIL ACTION - Burden of proof is preponderance of evidence. If a retailer has stopped an individual for theft, with good reason, that is enough. Preponderance of evidence is much easier to prove.

RESTITUTION - "How will my company be compensated for our losses due to theft?"

CRIMINAL ACTION - A retailer must rely on the state to determine if he will receive restitution. If some sort of restitution is granted to the retailer, it is usually for the value of the merchandise. Due to high workloads or politics, a prosecuting attorney may drop a retailer's case, regardless of the merchant's wishes.

CIVIL ACTION - The retailer is in control of how to demand restitution from (through the civil demand process). In most cases, a retailer can recover not only the value of the merchandise but general, special, and/or punitive damages. Since it is the retailer who is in control, at any time a case can be dropped.

DETERRENT - "What provides the best deterrent to future theft in my stores?"

CRIMINAL ACTION - Although prosecution is a good deterrent, it is most effective when used in conjunction with civil action. Since criminal courts and jails are overcrowded, the chance of incarceration or serious penalty is virtually nonexistent.

CIVIL ACTION - Crime prevention is sometimes best described as crime "displacement". If an individual knows that stealing from your company will result in: 1. Being arrested 2. The retailer may recover the merchandise from them and 3. He must pay the retailer $150, he may avoid stealing in your retail establishment in the future.

CORPORATE IMAGE - "How will my customers view the use of criminal/civil action?"

CRIMINAL ACTION - Criminal prosecution is a necessary evil. Although it is a good deterrent, sometimes the retailer is looked upon as the "bad guy". Also, criminal action is a public issue. Since arrest reports are public record, anyone has access to the records.

CIVIL ACTION - The high cost of security should be passed along to the offender not the good paying customer through higher prices. Therefore, customers should be outraged if a retailer is not practicing civil recovery!

Unlike criminal action, civil action in the form of demand letters is a private issue. The offender is not fingerprinted, photographed and incarcerated, therefore the public does not have access to the records.

VARIANCE IN PROCESSES - "How complex is a criminal/civil action program?"

CRIMINAL ACTION - There are as many different statutes and policies regarding the handling of apprehended shoplifters as there are cities in the United States. Every municipality has different criteria retailers must follow .

CIVIL ACTION - There are only 44 different variations (since 44 states have civil demand laws). All that is needed to civilly demand is: a civil demand law in your state, a correct subject name and address, and preponderance of evidence. (Note: A certain degree of legal expertise is required to research civil laws, write appropriate demand letters and respond to inquiries from demanded subjects and their attorneys.)

The merchant, and ultimately the customer, must pay for losses incurred as a result of shoplifting and internal theft. Customers paid an average of $209 extra last year for all forms of retail theft combined. Civil Recovery can help offset these high prices and enable retailers to offer the competitive prices customers expect.

Common legal questions and concerns

<u>Case History Briefs</u>

When Civil Recovery Laws were first passed, the main concern was their constitutionality. In the following two cases, civil recovery laws were upheld to be constitutional.

In 1986, a case came to court in Oregon ("Payless Drug Store v. Brown") regarding this topic of constitutionality. This particular case involved a minor and Payless Drug Store was suing the parent. Some of the arguments were:

1) The civil recovery statutes are too vague.
2) There is no rational relationship between the level of liability and actual harm to the store.
3) The statutes are unconstitutional in regard to the status of parents. The simple fact that one has the status of a parent does not warrant liability.
4) It doesn't make sense to penalize an innocent parent. All arguments were rejected by the Oregon Court of Appeals. This decision was later upheld by the Oregon Supreme Court.

The ruling basically stated that the civil recovery statutes do not violate the civil rights or the due process rights of individuals.

Another case which came to court was Shopko Stores, Inc. v. Terese M. Kujak. This case challenged the right to demand for actual damages. The issues discussed during the trial included:

1) Does sec. 943.51 (Wisconsin civil recovery statute number) permit recovery of actual damages where no damages under para. (a) are claimed?

The trial court implicitly answered: Yes

2) Are the lost services of the plaintiff's employees who must abandon their other duties to respond to the defendant's criminal and tortuous conduct compensable as "actual damages?"

The trial court answered: Yes

3) Does the assessment by a municipality of a $67.50 (amount being demanded in this case) forfeiture bar a victim form recovering exemplary damages under sec. 943.51?

The trial court answered: No

4) Did the legislature in enacting sec. 943.51 intend that jury trial be conducted in order to determine whether up to $90.00 (a dollar amount figured for this particular case) in statutory exemplary damages should be awarded where all remaining factual and legal issues are decided on the defendant's motion for summary judgment?

The trial court answered: No

Most companies surveyed claim they are experiencing between 20-50% of demanded subjects paying the demanded damages amount. Grocery and convenience store operators report their recovery percentage at about 40%. Some merchants have experienced approximately 50% of their shoplifters attempting to give them a false name and/or address. Laurie Lacaillade, Recovery Specialist for LPS, Inc., states, " We recommend merchants verify addresses given by detained subjects at the time of apprehension, by phone, through the criss-cross telephone directory at their local library." If a subject refuses to respond to demand letters, the final option is court action. This is normally handled in small claims court for a small filing fee. If, after all facts have been submitted and the court rules in the retailer's favor, the defendant must pay the claim and any court costs or a lien may be attached on property they own. Jack Isaacson of Lurias adds, "It is important for any merchant to meet and discuss the appropriate state statute with affected local judges to familiarize them with the law before filing any cases." Civil Recovery firms provide standard Civil Recovery Program to all types of retailers. They also provide a "Final Notice" program to those retailers who have an existing in-house system. This type of program follows up on those subjects who do not respond to the initial letter as well as fielding the multitude of questions asked by demanded subjects. Retailers should exercise caution when implementing a civil recovery program. Each state law should be thoroughly researched and demand letters appropriately written. A consistent, fair program includes avoiding discrimination in any form or the appearance of" making deals." The use of funds collected by retailers is not usually addressed in state statues, but they are generally used to provide funding for loss control training, programs and equipment.

SUMMARY

Every retailer needs a shoplifting prevention program. The best programs are those that are basic and uncomplicated. Physical design, systems and store personnel are the primary elements of any effective prevention plan. Environmental design and layout of the store and its merchandise is the first place to start in reducing loss. Most stores display their merchandise in ways that are designed to induce customers to buy something. Many times, this practice runs contrary to good security. However, a happy medium between effective merchandise display and good store security can often be reached. The next step is the continual training and motivation of store level associates. They must recognize and react to possible shoplifters.

Store merchandise can be physically protected by restricting access to it or by restricting its mobility. Display cases, display models and cable tie-downs are examples of restricting the movement of merchandise. This is obviously not a very desirable option, but may be necessary. Visibility of merchandise is also very important in deterring theft activity. High-ticket or high-loss items should be easily visible by trained employees. Another effective physical shoplifting prevention method involves the use of electronic (or dye) article tags. The placement of a notification sign, the detection antenna and the actual EAS tag on merchandise serves as a deterrent to theft. Many shoplifters avoid stores that have EAS systems, security agents, cable tie-downs or display alarms. Would-be shoplifters often head to other stores that do not employ these theft techniques. Finally, record all suspected theft incidents for later use.

Good luck in your fight against retail crime.

REFERENCES

Brindy, J. *Shoplifting: A Manual for Store Detectives.* (Matteson, Ill: Cavalier Press, n.d.).

Cleary, James Jr. *Prosecuting the Shoplifter: A Loss Prevention Strategy.* (Stoneham, Mass: Butterworths, 1986).

Edwards, L.E. *Shoplifting and Shrinkage Protection for Stores.* (Springfield, Ill: Charles C. Thomas, 1958).

Fennelly, Lawrence J. *Handbook of Loss Prevention and Crime Prevention, Second Edition.* (Stoneham, Mass: Butterworths, 1988).

Hayes, Read. *Retail Security and Loss Prevention.* (Stoneham, Mass: Butterworth-Heinemann, 1991).

Hayes, Read *The Retail Theft Trends Report.* (Winter Park, FL: LPS, 1992).

Hollinger, R., R. Hayes. *National Retail Security Survey.* (Chicago, IL: Cahners, 1992).